# Seasons of our Lives

FAR FROM FOUR

KANCHAN CHOUDHARY

BLUEROSE PUBLISHERS
India | U.K.

Copyright © Kanchan Choudhary 2024

All rights reserved by author. No part of this publication may be reproduced, stored in a retrieval system or transmitted in any form or by any means, electronic, mechanical, photocopying, recording or otherwise, without the prior permission of the author. Although every precaution has been taken to verify the accuracy of the information contained herein, the publisher assumes no responsibility for any errors or omissions. No liability is assumed for damages that may result from the use of information contained within.

BlueRose Publishers takes no responsibility for any damages, losses, or liabilities that may arise from the use or misuse of the information, products, or services provided in this publication.

For permissions requests or inquiries regarding this publication, please contact:

BLUEROSE PUBLISHERS
www.BlueRoseONE.com
info@bluerosepublishers.com
+91 8882 898 898
+4407342408967

ISBN: 978-93-5989-622-9

Cover Design: Muskan Sachdeva
Typesetting: Pooja Sharma

First Edition: March 2024

# About the Author

*Hey dear reader,*
*I'm just a girl,*
*Living thousands of lives,*
*Who loves learning,*
*And is in love with little things,*
*Trying to make people see their beautiful self.*
*I'm an empathic, silly, compassionate,*
*And sometimes a procrastinating 22 years old kid.*
*Content in my small world,*
*I come from Abohar, Punjab.*
*A city developing with a beautiful spark,*
*With people from all walks of the society,*
*Kind, jolly, intellectual, creative and everything mighty,*
*I've had my doubts while making decisions academically,*
*At each and every step,*
*But God has always pacified me to comprehend chronology,*
*And Destiny has brought me closest to my heart,*
*So here I'm, writing for you, embracing my art.*

# Contents

The Seasons of Our Lives.................................. 1

Little Things .................................................. 3

I Keep Running Away...................................... 4

My World's Falling Apart ................................ 5

Rainbow and You ........................................... 6

But What If Love Finds You?........................... 7

A War with Myself.......................................... 8

The Sun and The Moon in Me ........................ 9

Just Friends.................................................... 10

Universe Couldn't Save Me............................. 13

I Unintentionally Hurt Them ........................... 14

Him................................................................ 15

Distance.......................................................... 17

Even You Left ................................................ 19

I Fear Attachments ......................................... 20

I Grew Up Fast............................................... 21

Chameleon ..................................................... 23

Dreams .......................................................... 24

You Were the Firefly ...................................... 25

Metamorphosis................................................ 27

| | |
|---|---|
| Childhood | 28 |
| School and College Friends | 29 |
| Lies | 30 |
| I am a Tree | 31 |
| Untrustworthy | 32 |
| Thank You for Staying | 34 |
| Forever Patterns | 35 |
| Your Touch | 37 |
| I Watered A Succulent | 38 |
| Thanks To You | 39 |
| Adulthood | 41 |
| Forbidden Love | 42 |
| I No More Yearn to Bleed | 43 |
| No One's Coming to Save You | 44 |
| My World Ended That Day | 45 |
| Expectations | 47 |
| Your Eyes | 49 |
| Long Lost Friend | 51 |
| Did You Find Love? | 52 |
| Void | 53 |
| Selfish Realizations | 54 |
| Greenest Flag | 55 |
| Querencia | 57 |

| | |
|---|---|
| Yet Again | 58 |
| I Forgave Them | 59 |
| Love | 60 |
| Disrespect Will Never Thrive | 63 |
| Is This My Fate? | 64 |
| Hatred Requires Healing | 65 |
| My Dear Heart | 67 |
| What Is It? | 68 |
| Depression | 69 |
| Let It Go | 71 |
| Who am I? | 72 |
| Who Hasn't Felt Pain? | 73 |
| You | 74 |
| Hatred | 75 |
| Grateful | 76 |
| Selective Kindness | 78 |
| Numbness | 79 |
| Is It Love or Really Nothing? | 80 |
| Authority | 81 |
| I Killed Her | 83 |
| You're Enough | 84 |
| The Angel I Met | 87 |
| Destiny | 88 |

| | |
|---|---|
| *Dear Best Friend* | 89 |
| *I No Longer Have Energy* | 91 |
| *Anxiety* | 92 |
| *Your Care for Me* | 93 |
| *Confronting Past* | 94 |
| *I Was Mean* | 95 |
| *Manifestation* | 96 |
| *Festivals Are No Longer Same* | 97 |
| *Hope* | 98 |
| *Which World Are You In?* | 99 |
| *All I Wish For* | 103 |
| *She's White* | 104 |
| *I Wished I Was Dead* | 105 |
| *Random Thoughts Afloat* | 107 |
| *It's A Defense Mechanism* | 108 |
| *A Traumatized Child* | 109 |
| *My Heart Yearns for Your Heart* | 110 |
| *Forgiveness* | 111 |
| *Fulfillment* | 112 |
| *Dear Self* | 113 |
| *Our Seasons Are Endless* | 114 |

# The Seasons of Our Lives

*Our seasons are far from four,*

*Those instilled in our heart's core,*

*From feeling everything so deeply; like scratching wounds,*

*To feeling nothing at all; like when there's no moon.*

*From throwing away vases, to sitting drenched in water glasses.*

*From jumping to boundaries unknown, to not being able to move at all.*

*From spitting out every random thought, to holding even the loudest notes.*

*From flying through the rainbows, to hindered by thunderous clouds.*

*From being at the top of the world to equally beneath the ground.*

*These seasons are endless and there's no way their depths can be calibrated,*

*It's our feelings and emotions that make them feel celebrated.*

# Little Things

*The marmoris unfolded by the sunshine,*

*The tranquilizing petrichor emanating after the rain,*

*The little kid jumping ecstatically to be carried on father's shoulders,*

*The kindness of people in the middle of catastrophic disasters,*

*The smiles of patients,*

*The tyndall effect through the canopy of the wild,*

*The dancing particles in that beam of light,*

*And the courage of people thriving through their plight,*

*All these colors of the rainbow,*

*Pour into my sky,*

*These little things aren't so little,*

*They hold the capacity to somehow fix even the abysses in my heart,*

*These not so little phenomenons act as nepenthe,*

*And let my sufferings momentarily suppress.*

# I Keep Running Away

*Why do I keep running away,*
*I run from the people who act as an elixir for my soul,*
*Who care for me when I need it the most,*
*I keep pushing them away due to my neurological controls,*
*Which are often perplexed whether to stay or leave the possible paradise,*
*Perhaps I'm afraid they would come so close,*
*And discover my wounds,*
*They may end up detecting my pain,*
*And will eventually leave,*
*Or maybe I'm bothered by the society,*
*Who would eventually blame me for merely living,*
*No, actually it's because I'm convinced,*
*That in the end it isn't going to work out,*
*And I would be abandoned to ultimately grieve.*

# My World's Falling Apart

*The world's falling apart,*
*Skyscrapers crashing,*
*All the stars falling down,*
*Every substance is disintegrating into pieces,*
*As minute as an atom,*
*The drought ridden areas are flooding,*
*And the voids are growing deeper in each dimension,*
*Each substance is on a swirl,*
*But why couldn't you figure out,*
*It's me,*
*I'm the world.*

# Rainbow and You

*You were the rainbow I needed,*
*After the rain that bleeded,*
*I thought you came,*
*You did but with a dash of tint,*
*I hoped it would shine bright,*
*You instead diminished your vibrant light,*
*And now I'm left here alone without your sight.*

# But What If Love Finds You?

*What if after all these years of trail,*
*Thousand of disappointments,*
*And a zillion moments of self-doubt,*
*Love bestows upon you,*
*And all your voids begin to refill,*
*The million pieces of your heart fall back in place,*
*All the cracks in your bones finally find light,*
*And each muscle of yours feels warmth,*
*And then love complains,*
*"I've been looking for you,*
*Why have you been running away?"*

# A War with Myself

*I'm in a persistent war,*
*Fighting against myself inside my brain,*
*Every single day,*
*My neurons strive hard to work efficiently,*
*I really don't wish to be here,*
*But it's my tragedy,*
*For I'm trapped since forever,*
*I've tried escaping,*
*Unfortunately this maze is too tangled for me to find a way out,*
*Consequently I live in this abode with my twisted neurons constantly coiling around.*

# The Sun and The Moon in Me

*The sun and the moon inside me,*
*Often bewilder me about all of my existence,*
*I'm the light, a ray of hope,*
*But not sure if I'm meant to burn; quite like the sun,*
*Or be the sigh for the world in the form of moonlight,*
*Glistening in each phase.*

# Just Friends

*You call me all the sweet names,*
*You create all the poetic rhymes for me,*
*We exchange every minute detail of the day,*
*Are we really just friends?*

*We stand strong beside each other during gales,*
*And become robust shelters during torrential rains,*
*You wait for me till I get my chores done,*
*I consciously wait for your notification to pop up,*
*We yearn to have a conversation,*
*Are we still just friends?*

*Mornings begin with the thought of you,*
*Evenings aren't complete without hearing your melodious voice,*
*You text 'good morning' everyday,*
*And convince me to talk to you round the clock,*
*Yet "friends" is what we're called.*

*You say you could give up your life for me,*
*And that your heart already belongs to me,*
*You alchemize our every miniscule detail,*
*Yet Friendship is what we really share?*

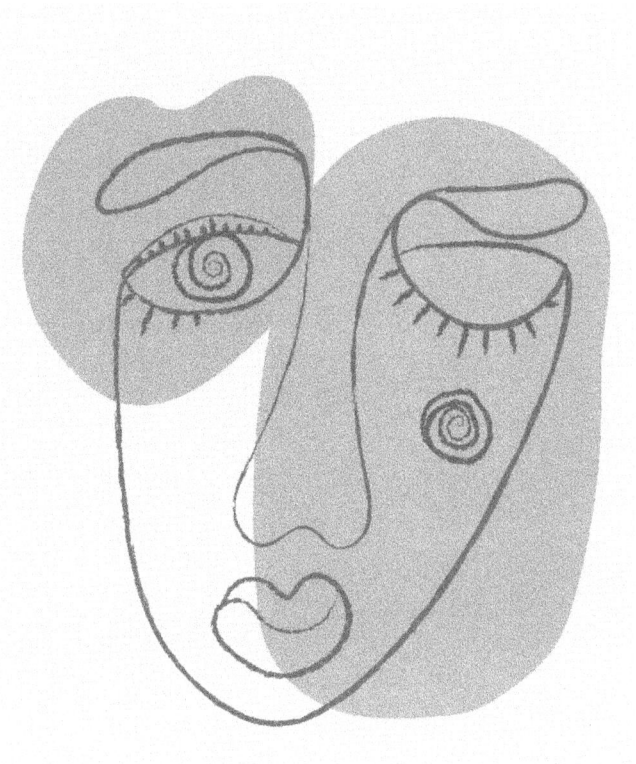

# Universe Couldn't Save Me

*The universe couldn't save me,*
*What wrong did I do to deserve such fate?*
*Naïve enough to know a thing,*
*Why couldn't anyone redeem me from such a sting?*
*The one that's always hurting,*
*The one who's scar is never fading,*
*Why was there nobody to deter the barbarism?*
*Why weren't they afraid of the repercussions?*
*Why do I have to be their prey?*
*Will there be atonement of some sort?*
*Or did I do something so disgusting in my previous life?*
*To be worthy of such tormenting times.*

# I Unintentionally Hurt Them

*I don't wish to hurt any being,*
*But those silent battles in my head,*
*Coerce me to break through my patience,*
*So while i strive to conceal my pain,*
*I end up hurting them,*
*And all my efforts go in vain.*

# Him

*I fell in love,*
*I have no clue; why, when and how I fell for him,*
*But I did,*
*I fell so deep,*
*Deep enough that it's quite impossible for me to step out now,*
*It was so sudden,*
*Just the way this poem begun,*
*For now I've entered into a utopia,*
*A glittery magical universe in his eyes,*
*I can deny my love but I can't deny the depth of his eyes,*
*Where I can swim for days and nights,*
*Without even blinking,*
*I just wish to drown in his intense oceanic eyes,*
*I may not know swimming,*
*For it would assist me to utterly sink in.*

# Distance

*We must be a thousand miles away,*
*Distance could never be an obstacle,*
*For when hearts are bound magically in conjunction,*
*Even if the universe conspires to break us apart,*
*There are legion neural pathways,*
*That would still paint your picture in my heart.*

# Even You Left

*You made my heart smile,*
*You released me from my pain,*
*You faded my scars,*
*You watered my dead flowers,*
*You let me witness my sapphires,*
*But eventually even you parted ways,*
*And now here I'm,*
*Submerged in despair.*

# I Fear Attachments

*No, I am not scared of loving,*
*For I'm full of love to offer,*
*I fear attachments,*
*I'm afraid when people get close.,*
*Not because they would hurt me,*
*Rather they may end up examining my agony,*
*And would never be able to understand my suffering,*
*Lending me into a situation from where i need to evacuate,*
*And once again I would be drenching myself in the same dreadful rain.*

# I Grew Up Fast

*I think I grew up so fast,*
*As soon as I stumbled upon my past,*
*I used to be a happy kid,*
*Wasn't really aware of the cheap tricks,*
*I was just levitating in others' worlds,*
*For my own world wasn't quite vivid to me then,*
*But as soon as I entered adolescence,*
*All my demons grew gigantic and I was surrounded,*
*I still managed to survive though,*
*But I ended up growing,*
*Such that I could no longer act childish,*
*I felt sorry to express myself on social media,*
*Venting felt embarrassing,*
*And asking for help was not even an option,*
*I felt like I've lost something,*
*A part of me was missing,*
*But then god gifted me with a star,*
*Who sparked childishness in my heart,*
*And now my inner child finally felt at ease,*

*And I convinced myself to act like a baby whenever I wished to,*
*For it was the sole way I didn't need to seek love or validation from the outside world,*
*And now I could create my own paradise within my small little universe.*

# Chameleon

*It's me,*
*It's you,*
*It's us all.*
*We're all chameleons,*
*After all we aren't God,*
*We've our seasons,*
*Far from four,*
*So why wouldn't our emotions swap?*
*We're like water,*
*Feelings would effortlessly flow,*
*From the himalayas to the plains,*
*Sometimes flood and sometimes drought,*
*We are so much more than we know,*
*So yes, we're all chameleons,*
*We'll always be,*
*As if a movie's cast,*
*Sometimes in the middle of the jungle,*
*Sometimes at commercial and residential zones,*
*Whether a child prodigy or an amateur art,*
*It's all about the extent of our seasons' blast.*

# Dreams

*Sleep was once an escape,*
*Until a day,*
*It became daunting,*
*From 5 to 2 hours a day,*
*Initially, 'Bittersweet' you can say,*
*Later, ripping my heart into shreds,*
*I was frightened to sleep without hearing 'the note',*
*Horrifying dreams,*
*Anxiety, I couldn't denote.*
*Nerve wracking dreams kept magnifying.*
*I tried finding my way out,*
*But I would find myself stuck at the round about.*
*Petrified, had to face it all,*
*A fear is now always along.*
*But I know,*
*This isn't where I belong,*
*I've faced hardest of times alone,*
*To be shaken by such storms.*

# You Were the Firefly

*I thought you were the sunshine meant to stay forever,*
*I now realize,*
*You were the firefly,*
*Meant to light up my darkness,*
*Glow for a while,*
*And then abandon me,*
*For now I must be capable,*
*Yet alone and helpless.*

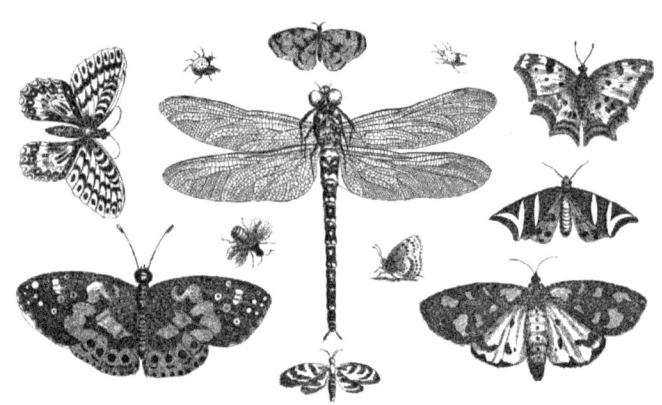

# Metamorphosis

*We certainly metamorphosize throughout our lives,*
*Resembling the butterflies,*
*They complete their life cycle in four stages,*
*From egg to larva to pupa then grows an adult,*
*Similarly we metamorphose as per universe's will,*
*For whenever there's a downpour,*
*Thus the flooded sites,*
*And we find ourselves stuck at that very site,*
*This is exactly the prerequisite to metamorphosize,*
*This is when it's time to move forward,*
*Towards the next stage,*
*To the next page,*
*To become the better version of ourselves,*
*And paint our wings in vibrant colors,*
*But since even colors loose a tint of sparkle with time,*
*So whenever it feels like your world's beginning to end,*
*Perhaps it's time to metamorphosize again.*

# Childhood

*Everyone says they want to live their childhood again,*
*That they would like to time travel to reminisce those memories,*
*I'm hesitant to say but I don't wish to do the same,*
*I would not like to live or even recreate those days again,*
*For I've just discovered myself,*
*Yes, I was happy during my childhood,*
*But I wasn't content,*
*I had known joy,*
*But something wasn't correct,*
*For my sub-conscious mind had known some other world,*
*The one I couldn't then comprehend,*
*But now I've realized it all,*
*And I've no option rather to acknowledge it,*
*And since I've been doing so for quite a time now,*
*I've finally found some peace,*
*The kind I had never known,*
*Therefore, I would never dare to wish for time to rewind,*
*And even if I appear as an outcast to admit it,*
*I would never wish to live my childhood again.*

# School and College Friends

*There was always a house,*
*Not just one; many,*
*Some of them were part of a greater abode,*
*Each had its own color,*
*A distinct trait,*
*One appeared red, other green, one white and even black,*
*There were legion,*
*And I couldn't choose either,*
*I loved each one of these,*
*I adored and appreciated them all,*
*I'm not sure how but I could see their VIBGYOR,*
*I wished all these housed to be homogenized,*
*To embrace each others' every shade,*
*But It took me a while to realize,*
*Every flower requires its own growing space,*
*There sustainability relied on trust and honesty,*
*They endured and fought against pesticides as a unit,*
*For now most of the houses have perished away,*
*Some are still intact,*
*But no matter their present surroundings,*
*They still hold universes within them,*
*And I still love them all.*

# Lies

*Here's a thing about lies,*
*White or black; they all fly,*
*Innocent souls will believe anything a liar implies; that's the irony of a lie,*
*Lies from unknown and those we meet every day,*
*Everyone has lies to display,*
*Lies are what they have,*
*Lies are what they sell.*
*Living a life that's all a lie,*
*Yet they try to convince people - a kind world is a lie,*
*Lies are all around,*
*But sweetheart,*
*Lies will eventually be found.*

# I am A Tree

*Most often I'm a tree,*
*Lively, endearing and free,*
*Providing people with love and compassion in its shade,*
*Enriched with the sweet, generous, fine fruits,*
*Whether they're consumed whole or crushed to make fresh juice.*

# Untrustworthy

*I loved you,*
*And perhaps you never did,*
*I ignored all the insults,*
*Wrapped in your sugary words,*
*I couldn't see the jealousy beneath,*
*After all,*
*I was blinded by my trust,*
*Yet I continued to pour love,*
*Stupid enough to realize,*
*I was going to be questioned on my empathetic self,*
*Even the care and loyalty,*
*Yet I convinced myself,*
*To not let it affect,*
*But my dear,*
*You did it again,*
*And this time it's far ahead,*
*My conscience hasn't yet died,*
*So yes it did feed on my flesh,*
*You might not confront,*
*Neither you'll accept your truth,*

*But I've finally learned to firmly believe my instinct's affirmation,*
*So this time I'll have to choose myself,*
*And find courage to walk away,*
*In a hope that we both heal and find light.*

# Thank You for Staying

*I blamed you, hurt you,*
*Fought you,*
*And even manipulated you,*
*I tried every possible way,*
*To make you leave,*
*Quite similar to the rest,*
*Who left at minimalistic inconvenience,*
*Why didn't you?*
*You let me harm yourself,*
*You knew I myself was hurting,*
*I hated myself yet cursed you,*
*I was burning in my suffering,*
*And I let the fire consume you,*
*You didn't leave,*
*You stood by my unhealed side,*
*Smiling,*
*And that's how I knew,*
*It's something forever,*
*And that you're not going to leave,*
*For we're bound together for eternity.*

# Forever Patterns

*I could reach out,*

*I don't mind,*

*But that won't make a difference,*

*For I'm aware an octopus would always emit ink,*

*And the stains would never fade,*

*And even if they do,*

*The patterns won't.*

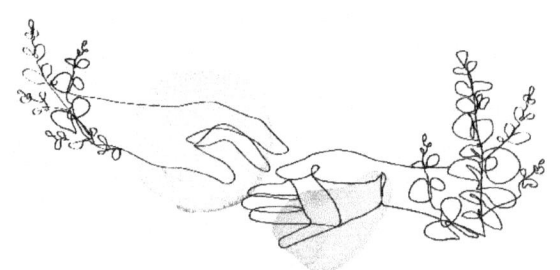

# Your Touch

*I took a walk in the nature today,*
*And amidst the chirping of birds and the empyrean surroundings,*
*The gush of air kissed my forehead,*
*It reminded me of you,*
*Soaring my hair like a free spirit,*
*Nipped my nose,*
*And a spark in my soul rekindled,*
*As if you said 'hey',*
*But in spur of a moment,*
*It passed by,*
*Quite like your goodbye.*

# I Watered A Succulent

*I watered a plant,*
*A succulent,*
*And Instead of water, it fed on my blood,*
*I watered it with immense joy,*
*But an uneasy joviality perpetually stayed,*
*So I abstained myself from doing so,*
*For now I fear what if I killed a plant,*
*The one which could even vegetatively grow.*

# Thanks To You

*All this while you blamed me,*
*You doubted my caliber,*
*You demeaned my aura,*
*I finally realize,*
*It really was me,*
*I was the light,*
*I was the star,*
*I was the petrichor,*
*I was the aroma of the flowers when they are crushed,*
*I was the fire and I was the ice,*
*Thanks to you,*
*For I no longer be blinded by your lies,*
*And Thanks to you,*
*For now I know you.*

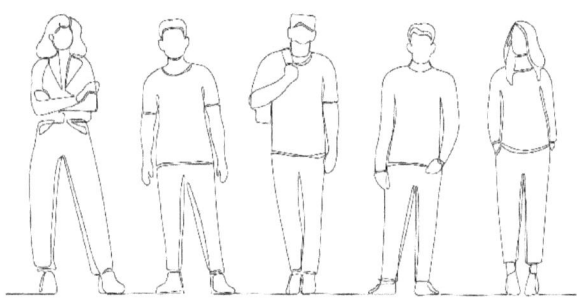

# Adulthood

*And sometimes I wish for you to be here,*
*For us to be together,*
*While reminiscing the days we were so adventurous,*
*Unaware of the adulting strings,*
*That have tied us poles apart,*
*For now we need appointments to see each other.*

*Preserving the façade of a perfect life,*
*Trying to be amicable all the time,*
*But the shadows lurking behind sarcasm create a sense of vexation sometimes,*
*But you still manage to smile,*
*Just like you did when your childhood ambitions couldn't survive,*
*For now you're inure to freezing summers and sweltering winters,*
*But you still blithely show disregard towards yourself.*

# Forbidden Love

*I never believed in the theory of wrong timing,*
*Until I found myself strangely rhyming,*
*I was naïve enough to go with the flow,*
*Later realized it isn't a star that effortlessly glows,*
*It would not be a long journey to be embarked,*
*Yet I desire for it to flourish,*
*Knowing my forbidden love won't be considered "correct",*
*For it might end us up in debt,*
*Well, there's no 'us',*
*But it would be a debt nobody would ever be able to repay,*
*Instead we might be consumed by it in one or the other way,*
*This isn't so banal or even acceptable,*
*Yet it did seem achievable for some reason,*
*I do realize now,*
*There's no such thing as wrong timing,*
*God unfolds the magic at the perfect timing,*
*For now I would be trusting god's plan,*
*And have faith in my forbidden love to be accepted.*

# I No More Yearn to Bleed

*I no more yearn to bleed,*
*For now I just wish to dive in the gentle sea breeze,*
*Curbing my fears,*
*Embracing my silence,*
*Replenishing my soul,*
*Hoping my heart brims with love,*
*And my constellations draw a pattern that you could understand.*

# No One's Coming to Save You

*No one's coming to save you,*
*This predicament where you've landed,*
*Is the culture media you must grow from,*
*Like a lotus blooms out of marsh,*
*It's you who have to mutate your icy soul into a flowy one,*
*Your static self into growing one,*
*To make yourself witness all the seasons,*
*For you're meant to be a shinning star in this universe,*
*The best of the mankind verse.*

# My World Ended That Day

*And one fine day my world ended,*
*Bit by bit and abruptly,*
*Summer still knocked on the door,*
*It wasn't even a minute late,*
*It didn't wait or stop,*
*My nervous system was abnormal for months,*
*And other pathways and processes followed,*
*The hot loo blowing during the afternoons dried my epidermis,*
*My muscles shrunk to death,*
*My footprints erased from all the paths I was meant to take,*
*And off those I once passed by,*
*My cells ran out of glucose,*
*And eventually my body was left with stored fat,*
*For now the moths and mites pierced into my bones via the flesh,*
*And even the butterflies I embraced turned into predators,*
*I maintained my calm; stationary and lifeless,*
*Until the predators got rid of the monsters engraved inside me,*
*And the things etched in the caves of my bones,*
*I couldn't even realize their presence until then,*

*Therefore it took months for them to scrap it off,*
*And set me free,*
*And then my world began again.*

# Expectations

*Expectations, Ah! Did it hurt merely reading the word?*
*That's exactly what it does.*
*After all human entities are meant to expect,*
*No matter how much we step back.*
*You think they'll change,*
*Did you start doing what you claimed?*
*It's been months rather years trying to mend your lazy ways.*
*And expect them to throw their red flags away?*
*You see their capabilities,*
*Their dark side will turn them into formalities.*
*See them as they are,*
*And not through your scars,*
*It's your story, you're the star,*
*Don't mortify yourself by expecting from someone close yet so far,*
*Expect from yourself and you'll never be disappointed,*
*I understand it's humanly near impossible,*
*Our mind responsible.*
*You might think this kind of power is inaccessible,*
*Trust me, you're capable,*

*It'll take one step, a day,*
*To see the magic just a blink away,*
*So please let yourself breathe rockstar,*
*And don't be their prey.*

# Your Eyes

*Your eyes make my heart flutter,*
*Feelings clutter,*
*They keep me on the edge,*
*Sitting, while sliding on the sledge,*
*Smiling, while my heart wrench.*

*The nervousness, the rhyme of every music beat,*
*Like the dancing rain greets,*
*Every second passes too fast, so slow,*
*Without uttering a word, we talk,*
*That's the beauty of your eyes,*
*The essence of your eyes is as such,*
*Several poems have been written without beginning a verse,*
*The galaxies your eyes hold spontaneously put a halt on my breath as well as the universe.*

# Long Lost Friend

*I do see flashbacks of you,*
*For you my friend are my favorite memory,*
*The one I no longer wish to be true,*
*For we've had our fluorescent times,*
*Until adulthood hit us hard,*
*And we somehow fell apart,*
*There's no one to blame,*
*And perhaps it's best to accept this fate,*
*For now I am too tired of being a pawn of your chess,*
*So I wish you the best,*
*But with a no man's land in between.*

# Did You Find Love?

*Not everyone is fortunate enough to find love.*
*The ones who did, know this bittersweet feeling.*
*The finest among all.*
*Unrequited, one sided or a complete love story,*
*They all have their own glory,*
*If you have found the one, let them know,*
*Because regret will never let things peacefully flow.*
*After all it's them who made your heart smile for no reason,*
*You found the happiness that was far from your vision,*
*It's just who they're, makes you the happiest,*
*No matter the aftermath,*
*What matters is, you.*
*You found love, you found it within you.*
*You found happiness, something to embrace forever.*
*You might unite or part ways,*
*But do not let it rot away, going the other way,*
*Shards of glass have always been in the way,*
*But are they even colossal than the unique feeling that stayed?*

# Void

*Perhaps I'm a void,*
*That couldn't be filled,*
*No matter how much I strive to feel fulfilled,*
*There's always an elusive leak,*
*For I shall always be held by some string,*
*Tied around myself,*
*That might just strangle me to death.*

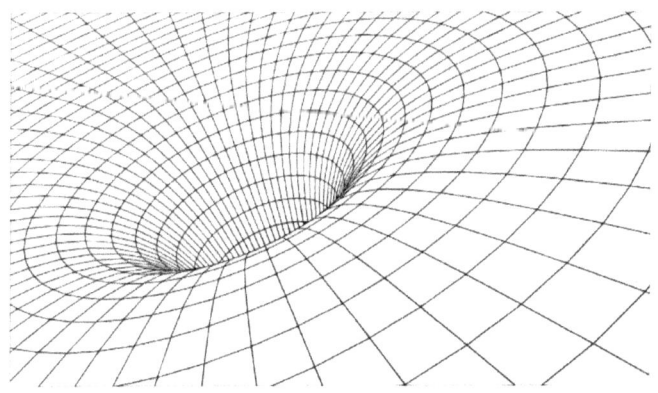

# Selfish Realizations

*How selfish are we,*
*What favors 'us' is all we see,*
*They did this, they did that,*
*Complaining,*
*Never mending our own ways,*
*Pointing fingers at others,*
*For what is inculcated deep in our own brains,*
*Accountability miles away, comprehension drained,*
*Arguments, disagreements, manipulation and ego ingrained,*
*We're the "evolved beings", as they say,*
*Perhaps for the sins that we propagate,*
*But we are equally sensible to introspect,*
*And confront the Gods and Demons within us,*
*Let our divine self burgeon,*
*And disseminate kindness and love.*

# Greenest Flag

*You my dear are 24 carat gold,*
*Whereas I am a broken soul,*
*I'm scared to hurt you,*
*And even about keeping my feelings obscure,*
*You're the winter rain,*
*Igniting merry in fields and on the faces,*
*Whereas I appear to be the acid rain,*
*I acidify the regions by merely drizzling,*
*And your smile as divine as your heart,*
*Is kind of a soul-soothing piece of art,*
*God created two of us too distinct yet so alike,*
*Except your childishness heals my inner child,*
*And I seem to be a red firefly under your greenest sky.*

# Querencia

*Is there a place I can hold on to?*
*Somewhere I readily belong,*
*A querencia where I can take a moment of sigh,*
*Where there are no if's, no why's,*
*Where the sky could hear my cries,*
*A place where my heart effortlessly pumps pigmented elixir in my bodily rivers,*
*And my soul knows fulfillment,*
*A place where I could feel the soft breeze embellishing my hair,*
*And the sky is teeming with rainbow flares.*

# Yet Again

*And here I am,*
*Enveloped in agony again,*
*All my utopian landscapes have fallen into ashes,*
*All those magical places I created somehow perished,*
*I'm merely left with my flesh,*
*For now the ants bite into my bones,*
*And the love I let the universe alchemize is imbibing my soul.*

# I Forgave Them

*I forgave them all,*
*But I couldn't forgive the ones who are considered my own,*
*"With whom I belong"*
*Since I'm not just hurt,*
*Each cell of mine dies every now and then,*
*Even my cuticles cry,*
*It's tragic; they'll never know,*
*I wonder how long will it take for me to be that apple tree,*
*Providing shade and fruits,*
*Even to those who'll eventually chop it off to fulfill their greed.*

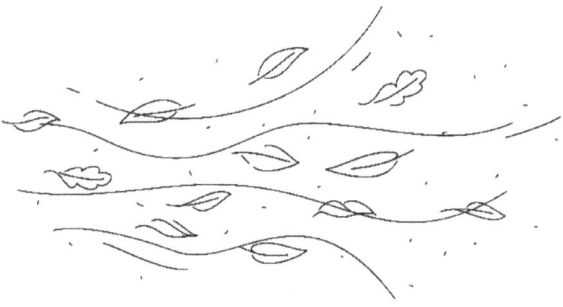

# Love

*Love is ubiquitous,*
*For every matter is made of love,*
*Every cell, every tissue is composed of love,*
*Be it nature, a cup of coffee, an animal or a human companion,*
*In any form, it's as pure as a dove.*

*Nature, the epitome of love,*
*Mesmerizing creation of the Lord,*
*For the stars, the rainbow, the sky and flowers are the ultimate shores,*
*To take shelter during a thunderstorm.*

*That friend who has been there in every thick and thin,*
*The one who laughs at our silliest mischief,*
*The one who notices our offs,*
*Who's our platonic soulmate,*
*Who turns every mediocre moment into something magical.*

*Siblings, our unpaid therapists,*
*The ones whom we hate as much as love,*
*Without whom the essence of life is lost,*
*For they are the ultimate love dose.*

*Our parents, who may sometimes not understand us,*
*Perhaps never be able to comprehend our emotions,*
*After all it's their first time living too,*
*Yet whenever we feel blues,*
*They adore us even after having no clue.*

*Love is all around,*
*It's not something we find once in a lifetime,*
*Just take a moment, look around,*
*There's love in each entity; profound.*

*Love is never wasted,*
*Love can never be an investment,*
*It's an emotion to be felt,*
*Not just once or twice,*
*But infinite times,*
*For every time you let yourself love,*
*A part of you will heal,*
*And every wound of yours would eventually find relief.*

# Disrespect Will Never Thrive

*No matter how much you try,*

*To make them feel seen, heard and understood,*

*They won't value or even understand your cry.*

*Leaving your emotions aside,*

*You always let your hurt slide,*

*And do whatever it takes, for them to glide.*

*They still won't respect it, respect you and your feelings.*

*Yet you do it,*

*It's you after all,*

*Kindness, empathy and compassion above all,*

*But sweetheart, this time don't let your self respect be compromised,*

*Disrespect shall never thrive.*

# Is This My Fate?

*Is it even worth living this way?*
*Until when am I going to be treated this way?*
*Is there an end to my suffering?*
*Why are my patience always overlooked?*
*Why does it always have to be me?*
*Will people ever find the courage to be?*
*Or will I always be blamed for my reaction?*
*Is it how it's supposed to be?*
*Is it what my fate is meant to be?*

# Hatred Requires Healing

*It's not that people don't have people,*
*Most do, but they themselves don't respect people,*
*It isn't always your friend who's a "snake",*
*Have you ever noticed your internal hate?*
*Those who try to help, you push them away,*
*After all in your world it's you who has endured all the pain.*
*You have gone astray.*
*No communication, no ties remain,*
*They gave you their all, talked and explained.*
*Your trust weak and ego ingrained,*
*Will never let you see the reality, not even inches away,*
*Take a break sweetie and give yourself some solace,*
*Away from the world where manipulation doesn't prevail,*
*Take the road of healing,*
*To discover magic in each and every grain.*

# My Dear Heart

*You're meant to pump the blood, how can you ache?*
*It's you who's hurt, why can't i think straight?*
*No electricity and you violently spark,*
*There's no fear no more in dark,*
*Why aren't you ceasing to ache, dear heart?*
*Ouch! It hurts.*
*Ruthlessly you prick into the muscles,*
*Fading my vision, my bones rustle,*
*My brain tries to distract myself,*
*And oh! it fails every now and then,*
*Cause you my heart aren't yet done piercing me apart,*
*Into a mess,*
*A piece of art.*

# What Is It?

*What is it that I can't figure out?*
*What's this incognito stillness about?*
*Drained in agony for a moment,*
*And optimistically normal the next.*
*What's it that I'm fine and not okay at the same time?*
*What are these thoughts that I can't define?*
*What's it that I am enclosed in exhilaration and misery simultaneously,*
*The beauty and evils of the society,*
*Like a dichotomy of some kind.*
*This co-existence of all my thoughts,*
*Is rupturing through my soul,*
*While I'm trying to comprehend,*
*All the lives I'm living and not.*

# Depression

*Something was off,*
*And I couldn't figure out anything,*
*I had no energy to combat so I just let myself drown,*
*I reached the bedrock,*
*And was held by the seaweed,*
*I tried to escape,*
*But I failed abominably,*
*For now self sabotage seemed the sole means,*
*A mere ray of hope was out of question,*
*So after a while, I let it flow,*
*Let the flora, fauna and everything around and inside me grow,*
*I practiced immobility until the seaweed released my soul,*
*I now realize,*
*All this while, it was the Lord,*
*Who was guiding the seaweed to maintain control.*

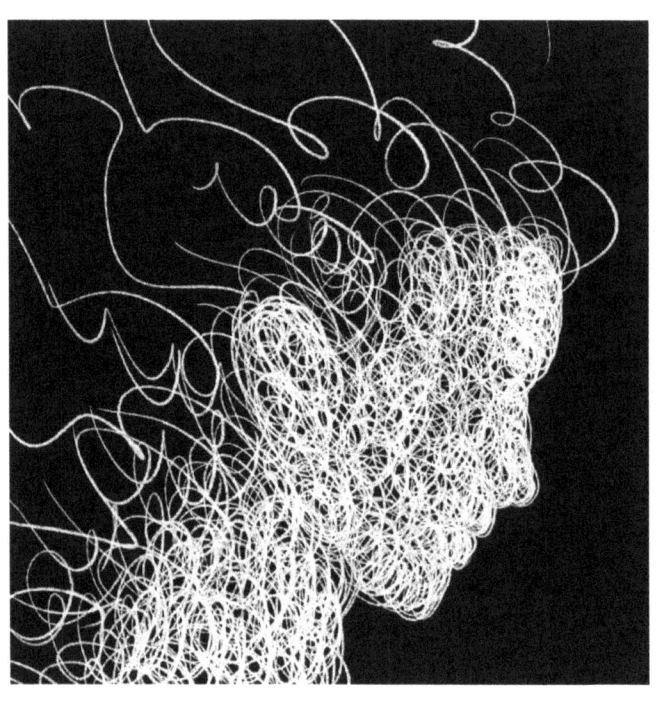

# Let It Go

*The tangled bunch of bottled threads,*
*Untangle eventually,*
*Strive against each other,*
*While riding with the breeze,*
*Striving and breaking,*
*One at a time.*
*Each bearing numerous fibers,*
*Disintegrating it for a thousand times,*
*From the very core,*
*Till the fibres unravel,*
*And the breeze stops.*
*Another wave comes and go,*
*Now and then, to and fro.*
*Eventually, they find a way,*
*To fly along the wind,*
*Broken and beautiful,*
*Ready to be woven again,*
*Into a warm sustainable sweater.*

# Who am I?

*For some I'm sweet and kind,*
*For some I'm mature as well as a child,*
*Someone you can't easily find.*
*For others I'm sensible,*
*Some even consider me wrong and evil,*
*And none of that matters when we know,*
*What we've been through, fought and overcome, all alone.*
*Not even let the darkness know,*
*About the atrocities we had to undergo.*
*But some questions still flow,*
*Am I someone who likes flowers?*
*Or the one who appreciates everyone's scars?*
*Am I someone you loves learning new perspectives?*
*Or someone who's drowning in the miseries of people who're depriving?*
*Am I the brave, patient, confident, bold woman,*
*Or a soft, hurt, compassionate young girl?*
*Am I someone who likes the moon, stars, flowers, smiles and the sky?*
*Or someone who's immersed in the love of 'Chai'?*
*Maybe, I'm everyone and no one,*
*Living thousands of lives, without getting high.*

# Who Hasn't Felt Pain?

*We've all witnessed tsunamis and rains,*
*We've all gone through some hard and dark times,*
*The ones where we strive to rhyme,*
*Some talk about it, others don't*
*Some explore it, others ignore,*
*Some are looking for happiness, others are living with it, helpless.*
*Some pulled themselves out of darkness, without letting the light know,*
*Some are fighting their way out, others are enduring their sorrows.*
*Some aren't even trying,*
*Whatever is the case, we eventually grow and glow.*
*We are all fighting our battles in our stories,*
*Fighting against all the evils in the society and those engraved deep within our brains,*
*Whether or not we win the war, the battle will be victoriously attained.*

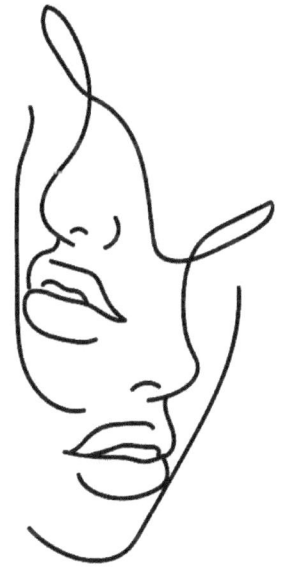

# You

*You fixed a heart you never broke,*

*You watered a plant you didn't grow,*

*Your heart provided the plant with immense warmth,*

*For it's you who introduced it to a wide array of flora and fauna,*

*You let it explore a whole new ecosystem under twinkling stars,*

*You smiled and the plant effortlessly flowered,*

*You transformed those pale leaves,*

*For now the plant blooms so carefree.*

# Hatred

*Hatred is all some have.*
*But there's light beneath that darkness,*
*The disguised glitter that needs personification,*
*Deserving of much more than our imagination,*
*A spark of compassion to ignite,*
*Like a baby bird takes its first flight,*
*As it spreads its wings at some height,*
*Realizing, it's capable of combating any plight,*
*Finding optimism,*
*And becoming so brave as it grows.*
*and then warbling a mesmerizing song,*
*"There's shine; more or less in every soul".*

# Grateful

*Everything, a nightmare.*
*But you my lord, were always there,*
*Sent the rainbow angels,*
*To get through those thunderous clouds,*
*Diminishing all my doubts,*
*As much I drowned in the ocean,*
*The angels; You, pulled me out,*
*I know you always care about.*
*You didn't let me drown,*
*My riverine brown eyes,*
*Could now see the lies and devils around,*
*Crystal clear and profound,*
*So vivid, that I could finally find courage,*
*To accept and forgive or to not be around,*
*To grow and glow, I'm not bound,*
*With no regrets,*
*Gratefulness is all that surrounds,*
*Grateful for the life I have,*
*Shelter and parents,*
*Food and friends,*

*Breathing and can move to any end,*
*Gaining wisdom, values and integrity immense,*
*Grateful for all of my existence!*

# Selective Kindness

*How's loving your friends and hating others, kindness?*
*How's praising your friends and degrading others, kindness?*
*How's pretending to be friends, later bitching 'bout them, kindness?*
*How's being protective about your things and mocking others for the same, kindness?*
*How's exaggerating your pain and invalidating others', kindness?*
*Is this your kindness?*
*Why's your kindness so selective?*
*Is it even authentic or just an impersonation?*
*My dear, please stop concealing your manipulation,*
*Your people pleasing behavior isn't kindness,*
*Deter yourself from perceiving so.*
*There a difference between being nice and kind,*
*Sweetheart, you better know.*

# Numbness

*No courtesy I've for you,*
*You didn't respect my honesty.*
*Disappointment slapped,*
*When you questioned my loyalty.*
*Bullies I suspect,*
*When you laughed off my morality.*
*Kindness I couldn't expect,*
*When you manipulated me over my originality.*
*Insecurity I detect,*
*When you degraded me for my sincerity.*
*Courage you don't have,*
*To acknowledge your inner cruelty.*
*You taking accountability,*
*Is out of practicality.*
*For now numbness is all that can be felt,*
*Universe's brutality.*

# Is It Love or Really Nothing?

*I tell myself it's nothing,*
*While staring at your picture and secretly smiling,*
*Cherishing your impeccable soul,*
*I reassure myself, "its just infatuation",*
*While I can't get you out of my mind,*
*You reside in my brain from dusk to dawn,*
*You have created an abode even in my sub-conscious,*
*For even my dreams are manipulated by you,*
*Yet I convince myself it's nothing,*
*But I'm scared all the time,*
*Afraid to lose you.*

# Authority

*All eyes on you and you're still doing everything inaccurate.*

*All the power with you yet nothing you can do.*

*All the authority you have and you still can't take those suppressing policies back.*

*How do you eat after snatching their food away?*

*How do you sleep after exploiting people this way?*

*How do you maintain your self esteem after swaying them away?*

*How do you face yourself in the mirror after lying to their face?*

*How do you find peace when you are reason thousands of lives ache?*

*Does anything matter to you or is your conscience too, fake?*

# I Killed Her

*I killed someone.*
*I killed her.*
*Over and over again.*
*I was her destroyer,*
*It was me, her biggest enemy*
*Nobody cared,*
*Why would they?*
*After all, I didn't too,*
*Self sabotage seemed quite pragmatic,*
*Moving an inch, impractical.*
*Laying down the whole day,*
*Watching the ceiling, without blinking away,*
*Each capillary of mine was twisting and twitching away,*
*And no part of the body could move any way,*
*I killed her.*
*I killed myself.*
*For my better version be born some day.*
*She had to die or else she would have been killed by,*
*For the light to enter through her cracked soul,*
*She had to sit and deliberately scrape her sores,*
*A part me still cries,*
*But no matter what, she had to die.*

# You're Enough

*There are people who save people,*
*You might be one of those brave people,*
*If you truly have someone, you're blessed,*
*If not, you still are; God doesn't suppress,*
*She'll show you the way; easy or steely,*
*It's you who'll have to walk it.*

*No one's coming to save you.*
*You're on your own,*
*And their impinged behavior your reward,*
*So don't let these glass ceilings have a hold,*
*Because you're so much more than what you're told,*
*You've been through so much,*
*No question is powerful than you,*
*No answer can hold the capabilities of you.*

*You are your inner self,*
*That needs love and respect,*
*Not from the masses around,*
*But from young, present and future self,*

*You're enough, you're phenomenal,*
*You need to start believing in yourself,*
*And once you start manifesting it all,*
*You'll see your magic unfold.*

# The Angel I Met

*Not a day passes by,*
*When your kindness and compassion doesn't strike my thoughts,*
*Not an hour, when I'm not reminded of your divine soul,*
*As warm as the apricity of the sun,*
*As if a song is being played by my favorite singer,*
*Feels like I've entered some fairyland,*
*In a world where love and acceptance reside,*
*For here I fly through the rainbows, riding on the clouds,*
*And the way you appreciate me, makes me feel so proud,*
*My heart has never known such solace,*
*Whether we are talking or there's just the sound of soft breeze,*
*The cute little creatures around us, adds up to the landscape,*
*And the vibrant, fragrant flowers remind me of your beautiful gait,*
*I know you have your doubts, your nervousness sometimes spikes,*
*But you still flicker radiantly in my eyes.*

# Destiny

*There are things we never thought we would do,*
*Or in fact, we could do,*
*But well destiny is the ultimate guru,*
*No matter what you go through,*
*God eventually leads you to what you're meant to do,*
*It's not about what's right or wrong,*
*You'll meet people from all walks,*
*It's about getting you out of your stronghold,*
*What happens is meant to happen,*
*Whether it's magical or something detrimental,*
*It might feel tormenting sometimes,*
*Trust me you'll be just fine.*
*Till then just hold on to yourself,*
*Because the Lord will never leave your hand.*
*But unless you yourself try to stand,*
*You won't be able to get out of this marshy land,*
*Just take a tiny step,*
*One at a time,*
*Don't be so hard on yourself, rockstar,*
*And witness your misery take a capsize.*

# Dear Best Friend

*He's a monkey indeed,*
*With a tint of humor but a lot strict,*
*Sensibility is something he has gained,*
*A heart full of love,*
*Which was once drained,*
*I hope you know, you deserve infinite love,*
*Coz you my friend are made of gold.*
*I know I can trust you,*
*As if a young bird trusts its wings during its first flight,*
*I just wish to hear your heart unapologetically talk,*
*I want to see you graciously walk,*
*I love you and I admire you a lot,*
*And this mutual love and support,*
*Is something out of the world,*
*Not everyone can comprehend,*
*Not everyone can withstand,*
*I pray for you; every now and then,*
*You keep a tap on me; whether I'm alive or dead,*
*This relationship is one of a kind,*
*Something not anyone can easily find,*

*I call him my best friend,*
*His place in my heart, immense.*
*For he is a blessing in disguise,*

# I No Longer Have Energy

*I no longer have the energy to feel,*
*My soul craves for some rest now,*
*I've been on expeditions,*
*But now I'm too tired to even whisper,*
*I just long for some ease in my breathe,*
*In the lap of nature,*
*I just wish to sleep,*
*Having no urge to even dream,*
*I'm just so tired,*
*And I've no energy.*

# Anxiety

*Each muscle of mine is twisting like a vine,*
*And my body is vibrating like an annoying alarm rhyme,*
*I am that annoying, weird vibration,*
*Perhaps I've lost my mind,*
*My feelings cluttering and blood is rolling around,*
*And my muscles are being hit by several hammers,*
*Installing iron nails inside my bones,*
*Neither I can sit nor can stand,*
*For I might soon collapse,*
*And this petrifying night,*
*Might just engulf me,*
*And I won't be able to resist it at all,*
*Perhaps all my strength is sucked up by some kind of a monster,*
*And therefore I'm turning out to be a disaster,*
*So much that for a minute, I am melting like ice,*
*And the next moment I may explode like an electronic device,*
*Perhaps I'll never see the light again,*
*Like I was never the child as was claimed.*

# Your Care for Me

*The way you care for me,*
*I just can't dare to lose you,*
*The way you know my needs,*
*Without even having to ask,*
*The way you understand my silence,*
*You notice every little move of mine,*
*You comprehend each detail,*
*I cannot fathom my life without you,*
*My nervous system faces an imbalance when you aren't around,*
*And my neurons exult at your glance,*
*I love the way you care for me,*
*The way you have always been cosseting me,*
*I love you,*
*And I love the way I don't even feel the urge to use my brain when you're around.*

# Confronting Past

*The daggers that once ruptured into my heart,*
*Creating cavities, causing impairment of senses,*
*Still pinch.*
*They were moved out and about,*
*Bent, rotated, rolled and twisted around.*
*My baggage was under control,*
*Until I tried pulling them out,*
*Blood all over the place,*
*Drenched in agony, I shout,*
*There's no one to hear my howls,*
*It's just me and my misery wrapped around.*
*I'm obscure, what to do,*
*And my thoughts are messing around,*
*They keep looking for a tranquil ambience,*
*For my heart to find some peace,*
*Far from dismay,*
*I strive so hard to stand up again,*
*And with immense bravery and grace,*
*I finally withhold my space.*

# I Was Mean

*I was mean,*
*I said something, I should never had,*
*I was so stupid to even think from another perspective,*
*And I'm accountable for being so subjective,*
*Trauma and someone's manipulation affected.*
*So dumb, I believed the society's stereotypes,*
*And later realized I wasn't right,*
*All these years I've gained some wisdom,*
*But those words still roam somewhere in my system,*
*I know I've realized my mistake,*
*But I still drown in the guilt of how i made them feel about their state,*
*I know it was something I would never say,*
*But I did, and I'm sorry for my mistake,*
*It's something I would never let happen again.*

# Manifestation

*This is the beginning of the magic,*

*Manifestation never feels tragic,*

*It holds power to transform our pessimistic thoughts,*

*And turn agony into hope,*

*It lets us prepare our own boat,*

*To move past the storm,*

*Diminish the yelps that float,*

*And turn them into musical notes,*

*To reach boundaries unknown,*

*Such that we finally believe in ourselves,*

*Find acceptance in each and every cell,*

*Manifestation is one of the best means,*

*For the heart to finally find a space with particles of warmth, serenity and faith.*

# Festivals Are No Longer Same

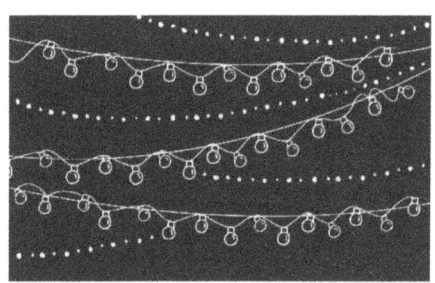

*Festivals are always brimming with joy,*
*Vibrant clothes and scrumptious cuisines,*
*The city embellished with dazzling lights,*
*And the people wearing sparkling wide smiles,*
*But my festivals seem gloomy sometimes,*
*I feel distant among hundreds of people,*
*I crave warmth in the middle of conversations,*
*I would be concentrating at each detail,*
*Yet I feel lost; as if I'm roaming around in other dimension,*
*There would be numerous dishes being offered,*
*But I would still crave for my comfort meal,*
*And out of blue, bullets pierce through my body,*
*Perhaps it's not normal,*
*But sometimes festivals detach me from reality.*

# Hope

*I just have hope to hold on,*
*For there's no one to rely on,*
*A shoulder to cry on,*
*A companion to laugh with,*
*A soul to embrace forever,*
*Or a partner to travel with,*
*I'm on my own,*
*Trapped in a cage i can't get out of,*
*I'm stuck with my elusive thoughts,*
*Held in chains,*
*I just wish to be free,*
*To refrain my invincible demise,*
*For I shall soon be engulfed,*
*But hope is my magic wand,*
*And the only ray of light which isn't biased.*

# Which World Are You In?

*There are numerous worlds within this universe,*
*Each of these largely diverse,*

*A world where there's not even food to eat,*
*No place to sleep,*
*No idea, for how long will they be able to breathe.*

*A world that knows nothing about pain,*
*The one which has never witnessed dreadful rains,*
*Where they do not let any opportunity go in vain.*

*A world where agony sustains,*
*Where there's no end to burning flames,*
*Where even the light is black,*
*And every bone is more than severely cracked.*

*A world where manipulation prevails,*
*Where people do mischievous things without any shame,*
*To fulfill their filthy desires,*
*And self satisfaction to be gained.*
*A world full of hate,*
*With hatred having no desire to escape,*
*Where divide and rule policy is the ultimate aim.*

*A world with blooming flowers,*
*Vibrant, captivating and fragrant,*
*So dreamy and heartfelt,*
*For their aroma awakens even the dead.*

*A world so numb,*
*Perhaps soon succumb.*
*For there are no means to clean the mess,*
*Because every cell, every muscle is under stress.*

*A world so lively,*
*With jolliness flourishing brightly,*
*Smiles so sparkling,*
*Like the twinkling stars.*

*A world so kind,*
*Might not be incorporated in everyone's mind,*
*Something you can find everywhere and nowhere.*

*A world with a void so deep,*
*Longing to be healed,*
*Wishing to find peace.*

*A world with volcanos erupting,*
*The one with extreme sorrows,*
*The one where livelihood is always at stake,*
*Living under the tree providing melancholic shade.*

*A world of taunts; degrading others,*
*Where one always suffers,*
*No matter how much you try,*
*The situation always streches like a rubber.*

*A paradoxical world,*
*No idea if it'll flourish,*
*Striving at each step to open new doors,*
*For the dreams to somehow glow.*

*A world of longing,*
*Switching between hope and cries,*
*Waiting to be reunited,*
*Waiting to be gifted for trying.*

*These endless worlds reside within our vast universe,*
*There's no way to confine these by any means,*
*They are seasons meant to come and go,*
*And yet flourish every time.*

# All I Wish For

*We meet people from all walks,*
*With kind hearts, pain engrossed,*
*Jolly and those having evil talks,*
*Having experienced it all,*
*I would sometimes wish to vanish into air,*
*But deep down I know,*
*Perhaps I just want to be found,*
*To be loved,*
*And to find someone as loving as me,*
*As understanding and caring,*
*To not hesitate of being expressive,*
*To be able to provide whatever my parents wish,*
*And to just stay healthy and feel fulfilled,*
*Sometimes this is all I wish for.*

# She's White

*She's the white light,*
*Composed of all the colors of VIBGYOR,*
*She's the white of the dove,*
*So divine,*
*Hurting her?*
*Even the devils wouldn't dare,*
*She's the white of clouds,*
*Her delicate robustness provides tranquility among doubts,*
*She's the white of the moon,*
*Radiantly shinning while embracing her scars,*
*And simultaneously captivating the oceanic waves.*

# I Wished I Was Dead

*I wished I was dead,*
*But I'm not,*
*Because I was tied with a thread,*
*The divine bond between me and my Lord,*
*Who was there to pull me to the shore,*
*With her holy interference,*
*Even my darkest scars found light,*
*And even after witnessing every kind of demon I finally wanted to live,*
*For now I'll live life to the lees,*
*Having faith in God and no one to please.*

# Random Thoughts Afloat

*What if the dogs cry at night for their long lost love at some plight?*
*What if the trees are keeping a watch on our "industrial wins"?*
*To later make us pay for our sins.*
*What if the ghosts are the aliens we're looking for on other planets?*
*What if Gods were originally "created" to mould our lives,*
*Probably, this isn't how we're supposed to live,*
*What if our ancestors used 'Gods' to turn our lives according to their will,*
*What if the moon eventually moves in the propinquity of the earth,*
*For all the hopeless romantics lost in its love,*
*What if this isn't even the real life we're meant to live?*
*What if the other side is where we are actually going to breathe?*

# It's A Defense Mechanism

*I romanticize every little thing,*
*It's something I do very often,*
*I wish for them to come thru,*
*Distance and longing makes my heart a grave,*
*I won't wait for the time of parting ways,*
*So I distant myself beforehand,*
*To alleviate the agony that would later come along,*
*I'm frightened of not being able to breathe then,*
*Therefore, I'm convinced to not involve myself in robust bonds again,*
*It's my defense mechanism,*
*I wonder if I'll ever break through,*
*After all, each of them will be long lost,*
*And I'll be sinking here under the weight of my thoughts.*

# A Traumatized Child

*A child traumatized,*
*Having no idea about wrong or right,*
*For he was the easy prey,*
*For the predators to sway,*
*Innocent soul, didn't had a clue of the demons around,*
*For now he persistently walks under cumulonimbus clouds.*

# My Heart Yearns for Your Heart

*So if my hope turns out to be delusional,*
*If you call it friendship,*
*And if our fate is not meant to be,*
*If the universe is unkind,*
*And If all this while I was blind,*
*Even if forever falls apart,*
*There must be a zillion reasons to not,*
*Yet my heart would still yearn for your heart.*

# Forgiveness

*The tragedy is, we've to forgive every being,*
*Even if they turned our world upside down,*
*We've to forgive those criminals roaming around,*
*Who once murdered our each and every cell,*
*Those tendons and ligaments which bled for so long,*
*Need some time to cure,*
*Blaming, cursing or self-sabotage wouldn't work,*
*But would add fuel to the fire ablazing you,*
*You must forgive yourself for the abuse you endured,*
*And probably those who put acid on your wounds,*
*And you'll be astonished,*
*To finally display florescence,*
*After being trapped in darkness for so long.*

# Fulfillment

*And after all these seasons I've lived,*
*And those I'm going through,*
*All my heart yearns for is you.*

# Dear Self

*Dear self,*

*Its time,*

*To finally know your worth,*

*And never settle for anything less,*

*And the more is where your heart effortlessly utters yes.*

# Our Seasons Are Endless

*Dark or bright, stiff or loose, crawling or flying,*
*No matter which stage we're on; in life,*
*Our seasons have to change and co-exist for us to survive,*
*One without the other has no meaning, no chance of hope,*
*That's why we have to bear with the scorching heat to later enjoy the snow.*
*Our seasons change too often,*
*And that's what makes us feel most alive; whether we strive or thrive.*
*To grow, we must respect whatever flows,*
*And let ourselves feel even the lows,*
*To later appreciate the glow.*
*Because these seasons together form the very essence of life.*
*So make sure you've felt it all,*
*Dreadful or divine,*
*You see, we don't have a long time.*

www.ingramcontent.com/pod-product-compliance
Lightning Source LLC
LaVergne TN
LVHW061552070526
838199LV00077B/7013